Mandala Colouring Book For Teens and Adults

The best practice of mindfulness

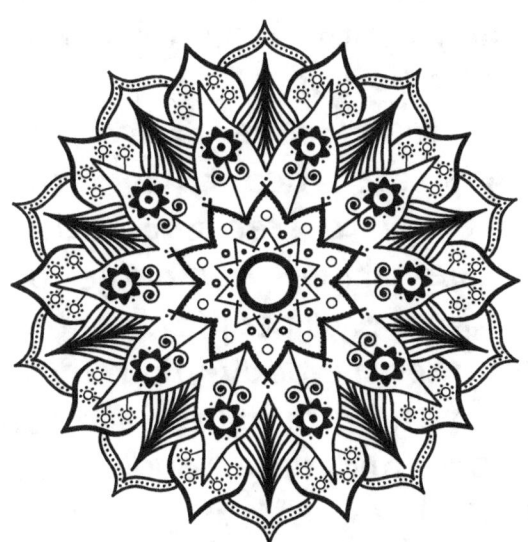

These beautiful 20 mandalas will help you to:
- find peace and relaxation,
- reduce anxiety and stress,
- be mindful and focused,
- overcome boredom and troublesome thoughts.

Submerge into the creative and artistic world while colouring unusual patterns using your favourite pencils or crayons.

by Le Grand Bleu

The meaning of mandalas and why to create them.

The word mandala comes from Sanskrit and it means circle. Mandala is a spiritual and ritual symbol in Hinduism and Buddhism, representing the universe. The circular designs symbolize the idea that everything is connected and life is never ending. The symbolism behind the creation of a mandala can have a significant meaning for many individuals regardless their religious.

Mandalas have many uses apart from meditation as the designs are meant to remove irritating thoughts and allow to free a creative mind within every one of us while we indulge ourselves with relaxation. Ultimately, people create and look at mandalas to center the body and mind.

The colouring of the mandalas is recommended for healing purposes and is strongly associated with reducing stress. It is perfect for those who suffer from depression, anxiety and restless mind. It also helps you discover your creative side which is often hidden and not realized of!

To colour your mandala choose any medium such as colouring pencils, crayons, pastels, chalks or paint - whichever suits you best.

To get started, it is best to find a peaceful space where you can relax and start the colouring, allowing any colour of your preference without analyzing it too much.

Also, do not try to match the colours, either. Simply use your intuition and instincts and let them guide you through the drawing process naturally. Did you know that you may use certain colours to attract certain things into your life? It is always best to select colours intuitively.

- RED for strength, high energy and passion.
- PINK for love, intuition and the feminine.
- ORANGE for creativity, transformation, self-awareness and intuition.
- YELLOW for learning, wisdom, laughter and happiness.
- GREEN for physical healing, psychic ability, love of nature and caring.
- BLUE for emotional healing, inner peace and meditation.
- PURPLE for all things spiritual.
- WHITE for spiritual focus.
- BLACK for mystery, deep thinking and individuality.

If you have an intention you want to meditate on, you may want to look at the meaning of the colours above and verbalize it on the blank page next to each mandala. Focus on the intention that you want to bring into your life and then start colouring the beautiful design of the mandala. The beauty of the mandala should absorb all your attention. Gradually you will feel more relaxed and even more intuitive thoughts may arise.

HAPPY COLOURING!

If you have an intention you want to meditate on, you can write it down here.

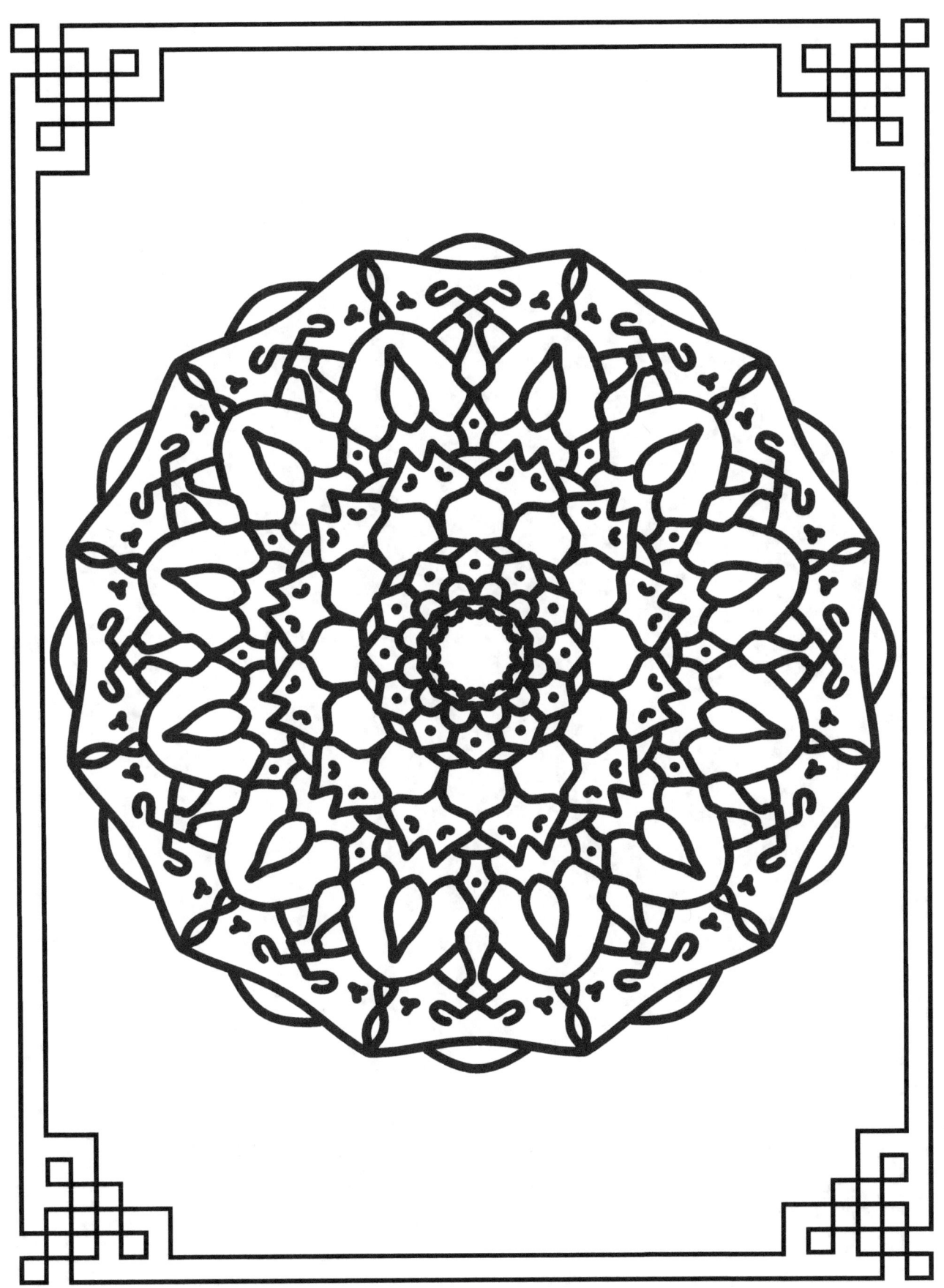

If you have an intention you want to meditate on,
you can write it down here.

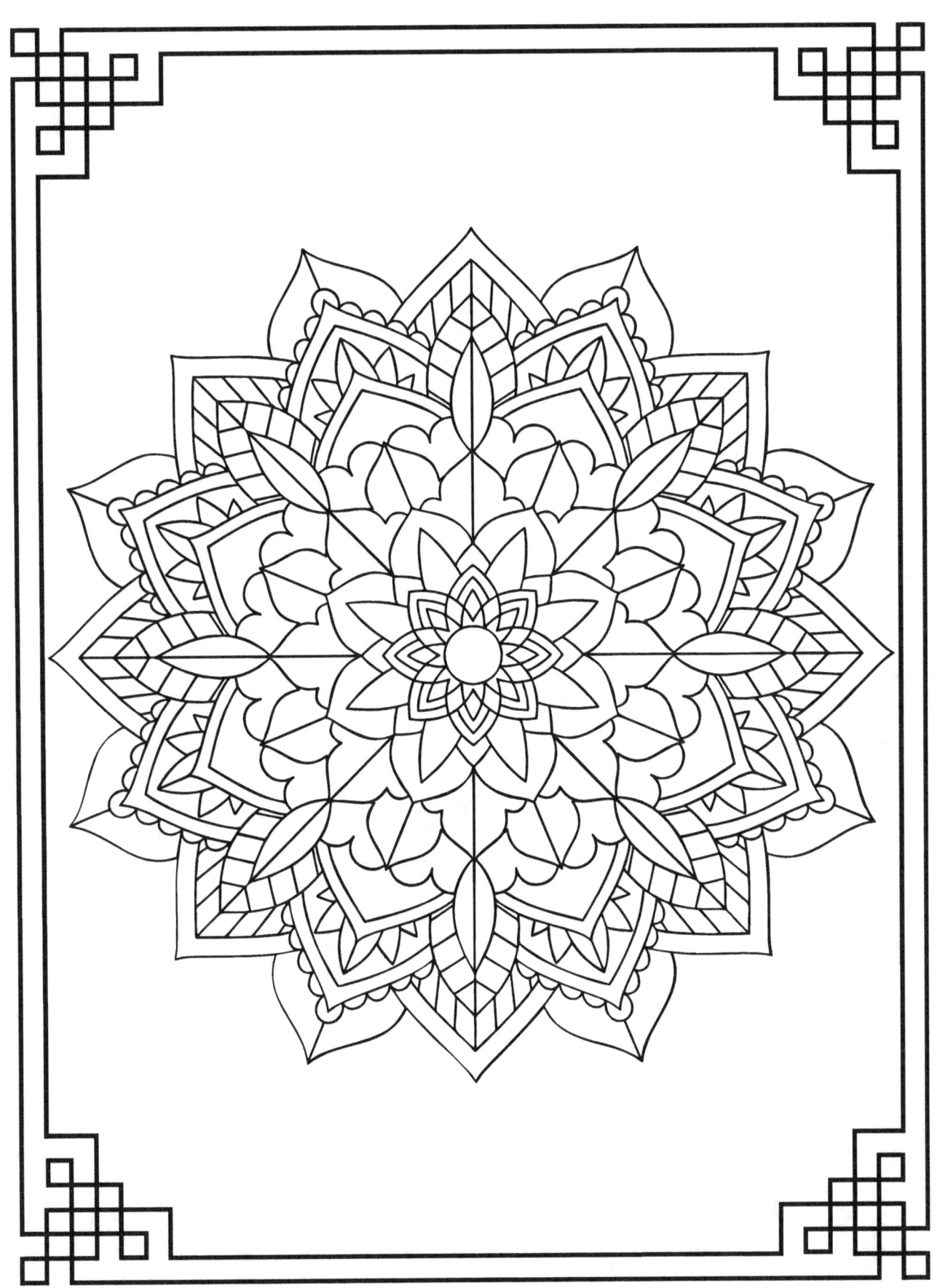

If you have an intention you want to meditate on, you can write it down here.

If you have an intention you want to meditate on,
you can write it down here.

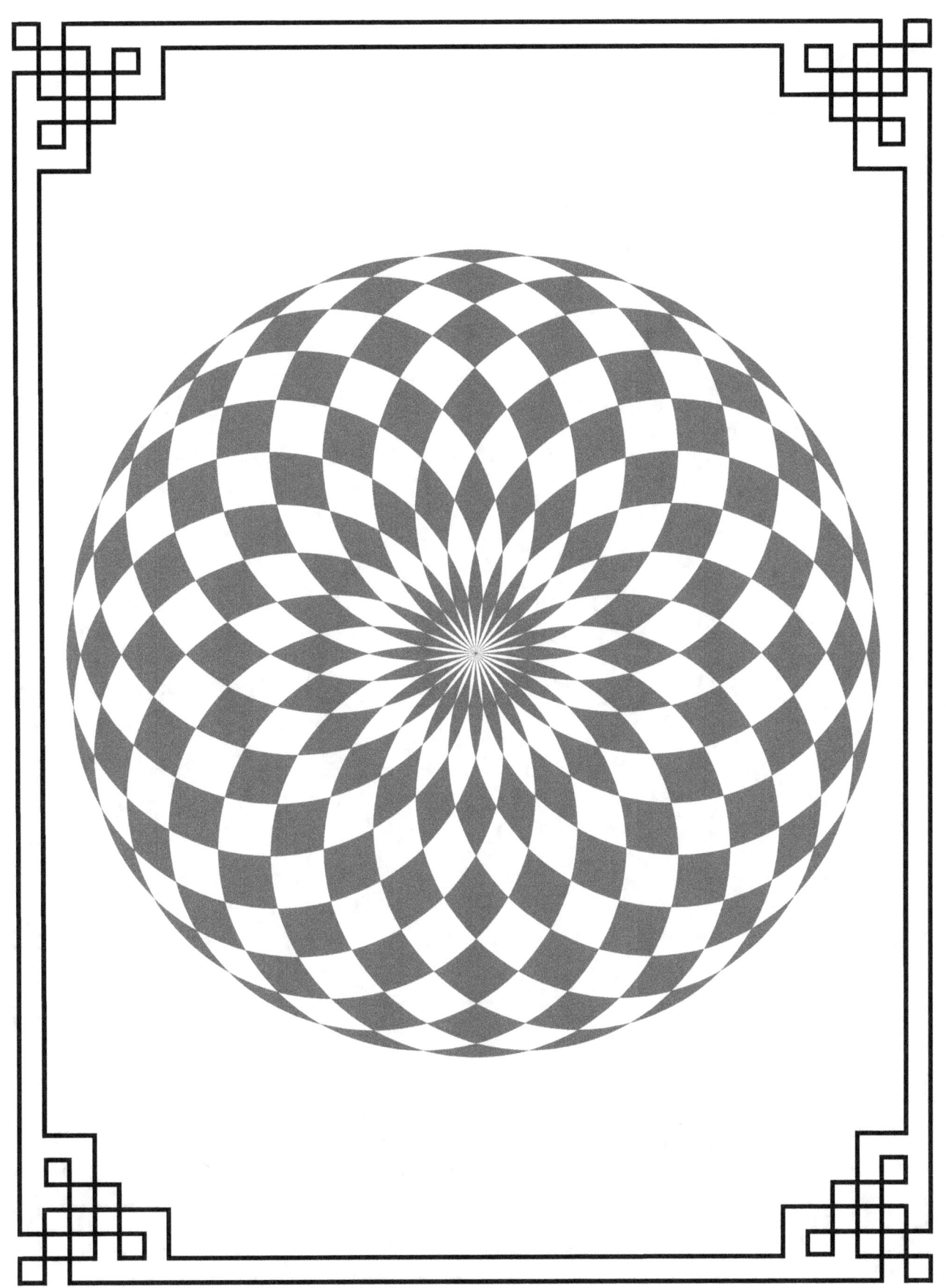

If you have an intention you want to meditate on, you can write it down here.

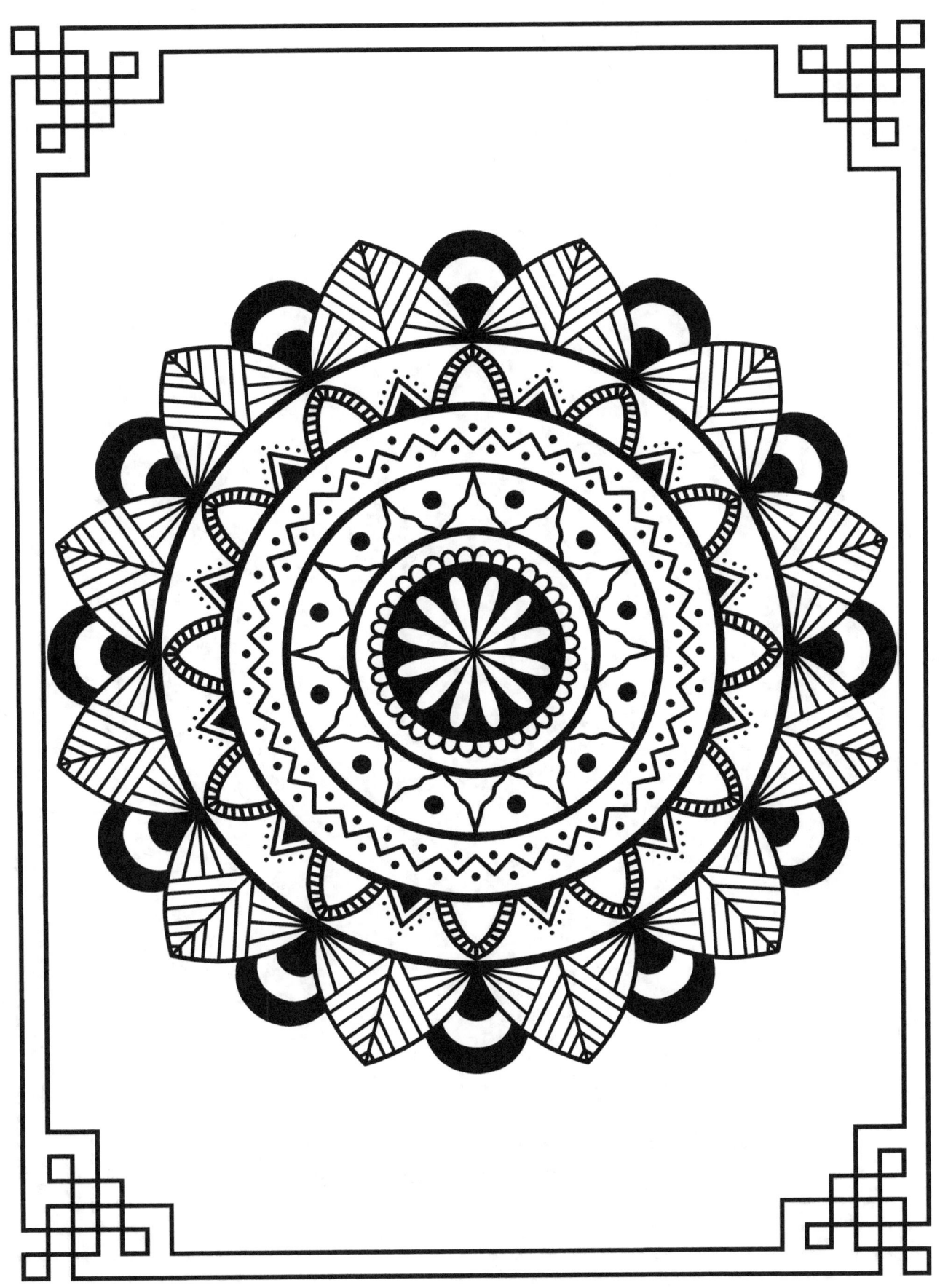

If you have an intention you want to meditate on,
you can write it down here.

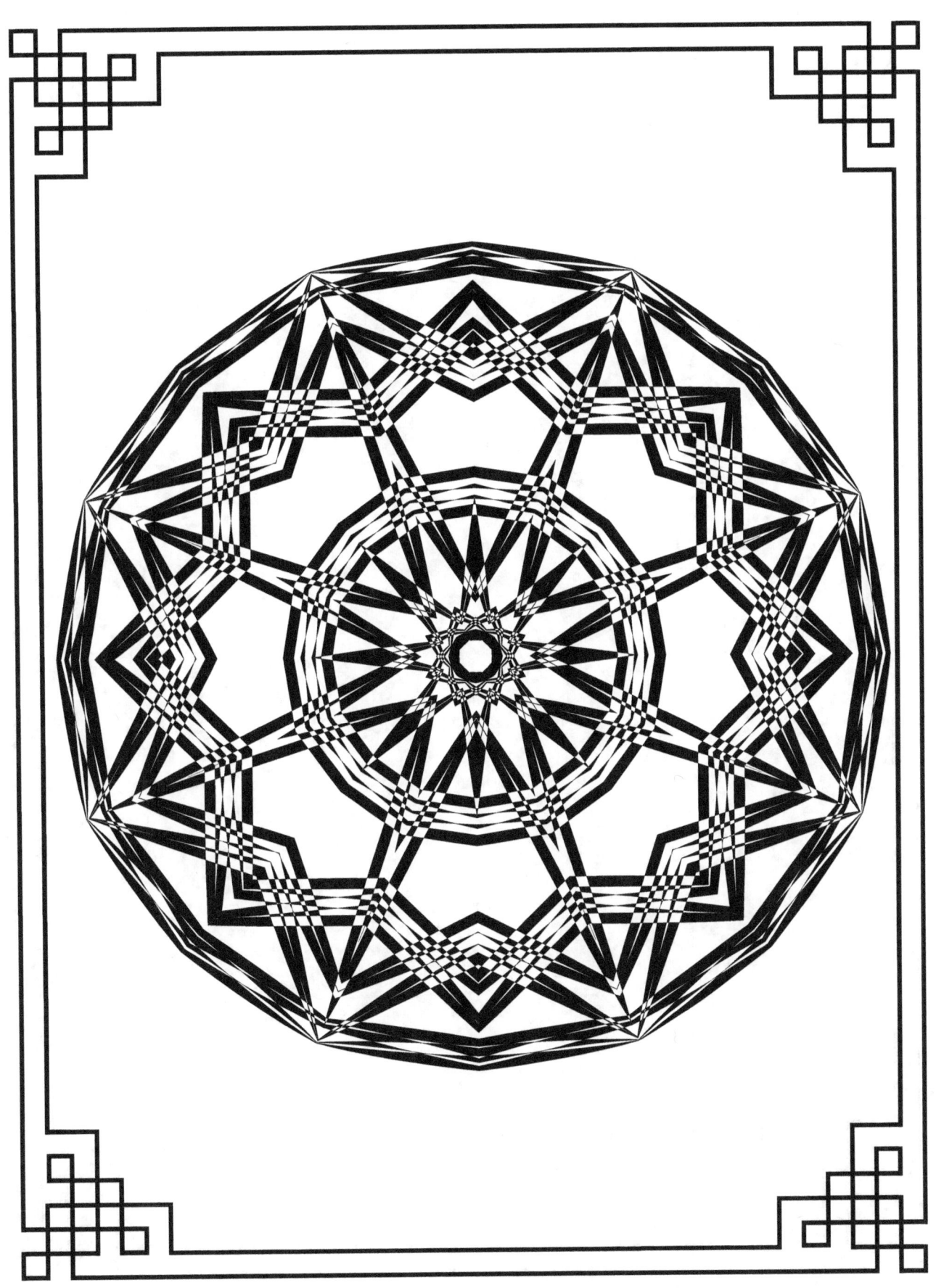

If you have an intention you want to meditate on, you can write it down here.

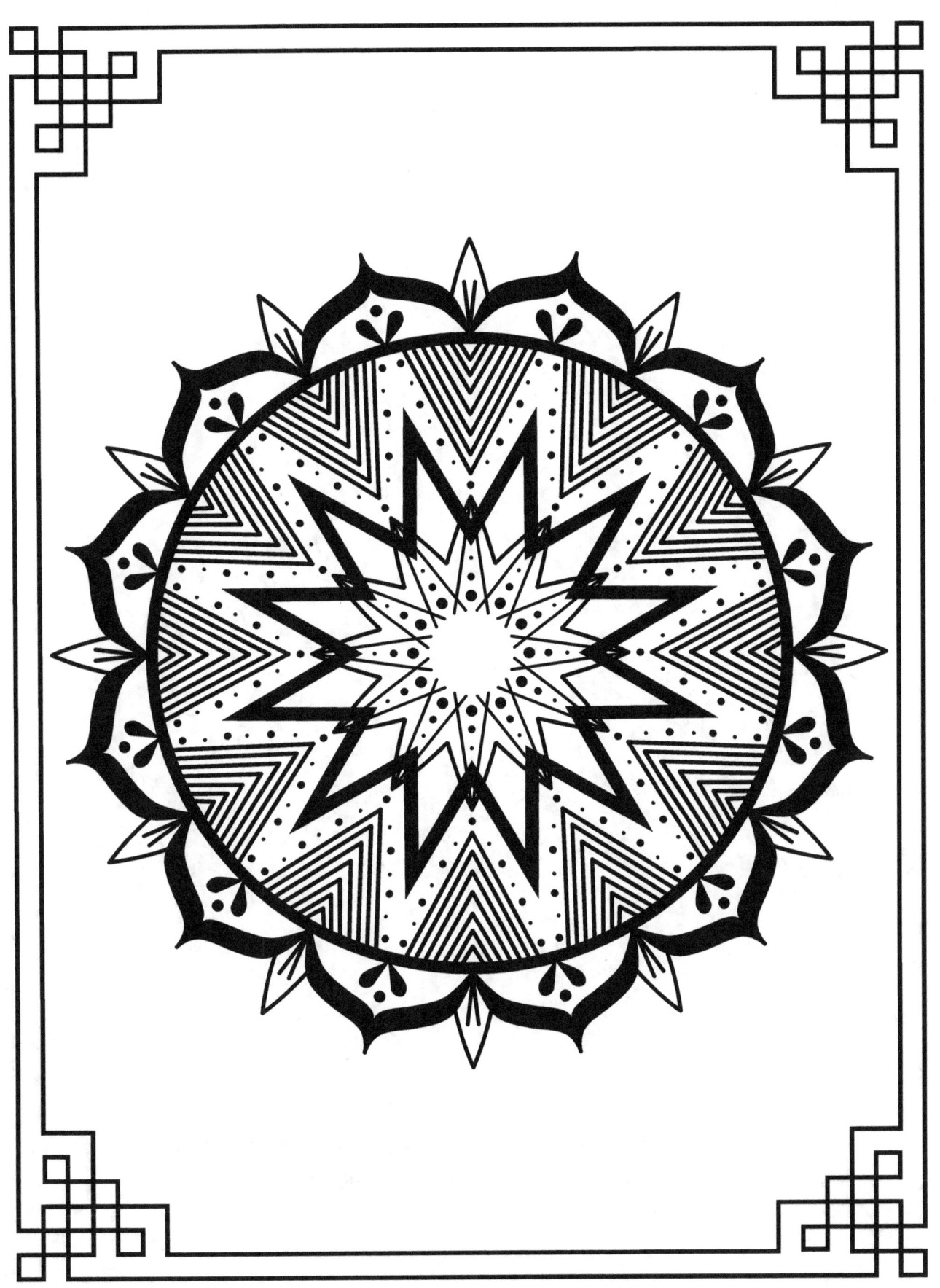

If you have an intention you want to meditate on, you can write it down here.

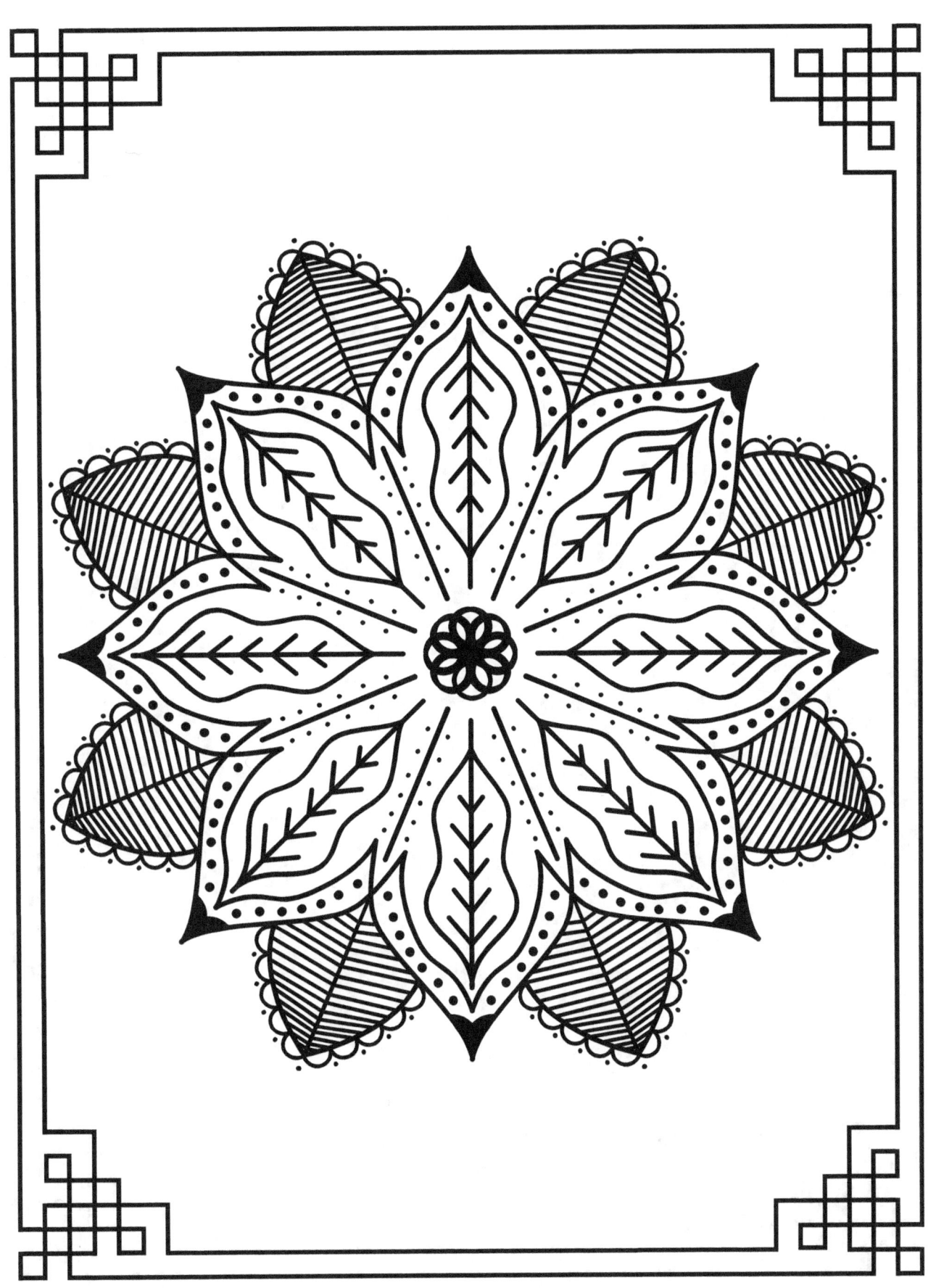

If you have an intention you want to meditate on, you can write it down here.

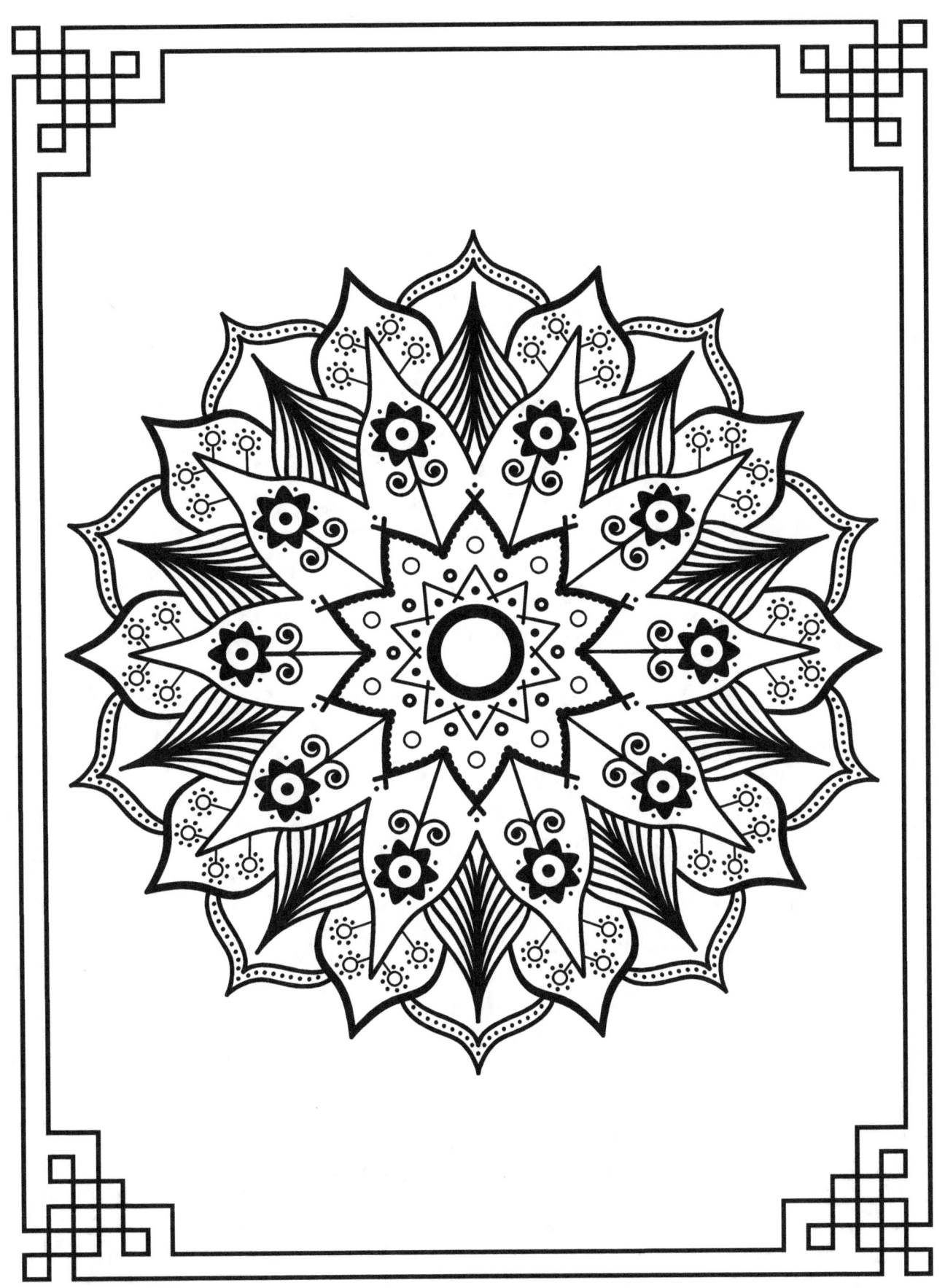

If you have an intention you want to meditate on, you can write it down here.

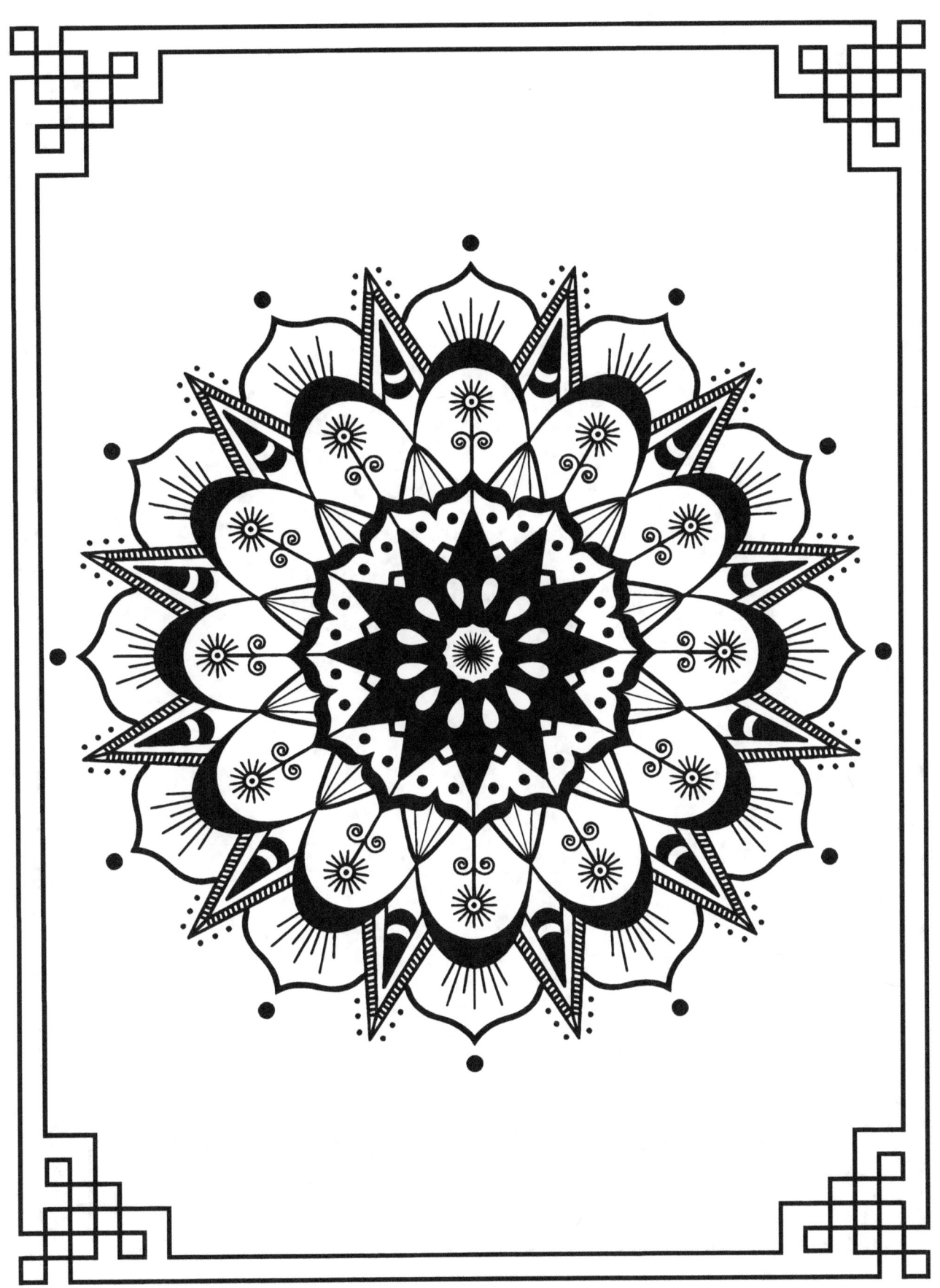

If you have an intention you want to meditate on, you can write it down here.

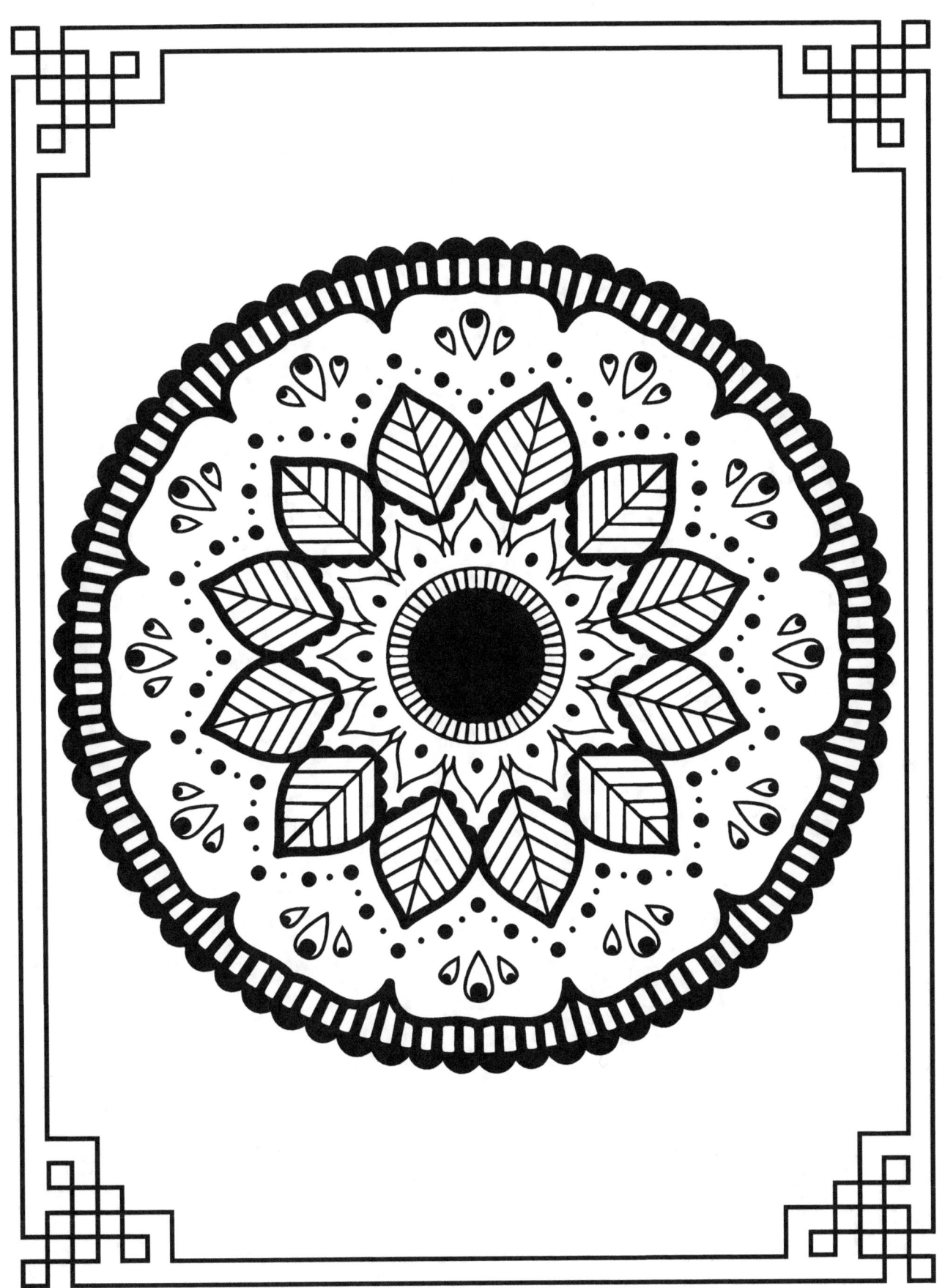

If you have an intention you want to meditate on, you can write it down here.

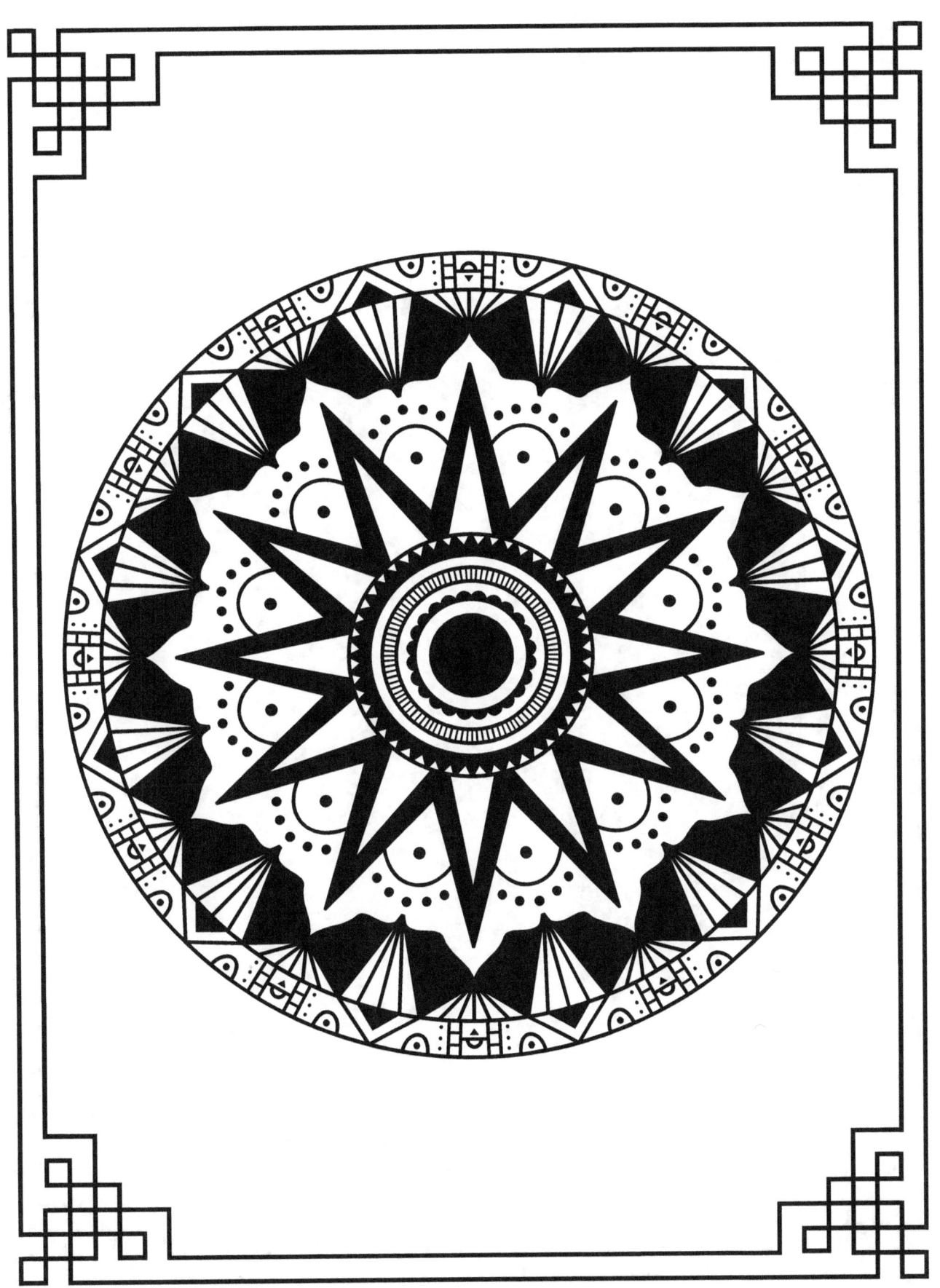

If you have an intention you want to meditate on, you can write it down here.

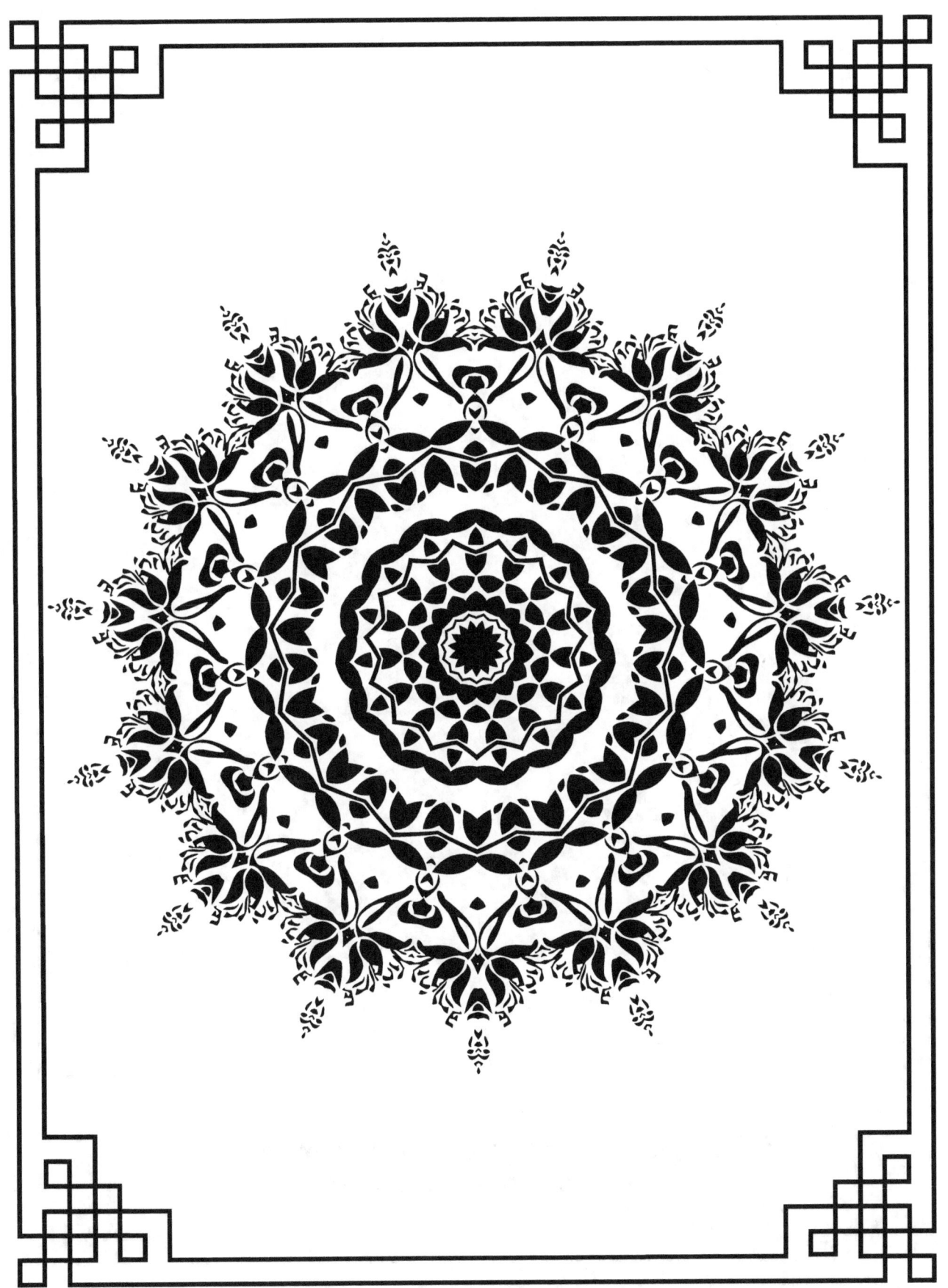

If you have an intention you want to meditate on,
you can write it down here.

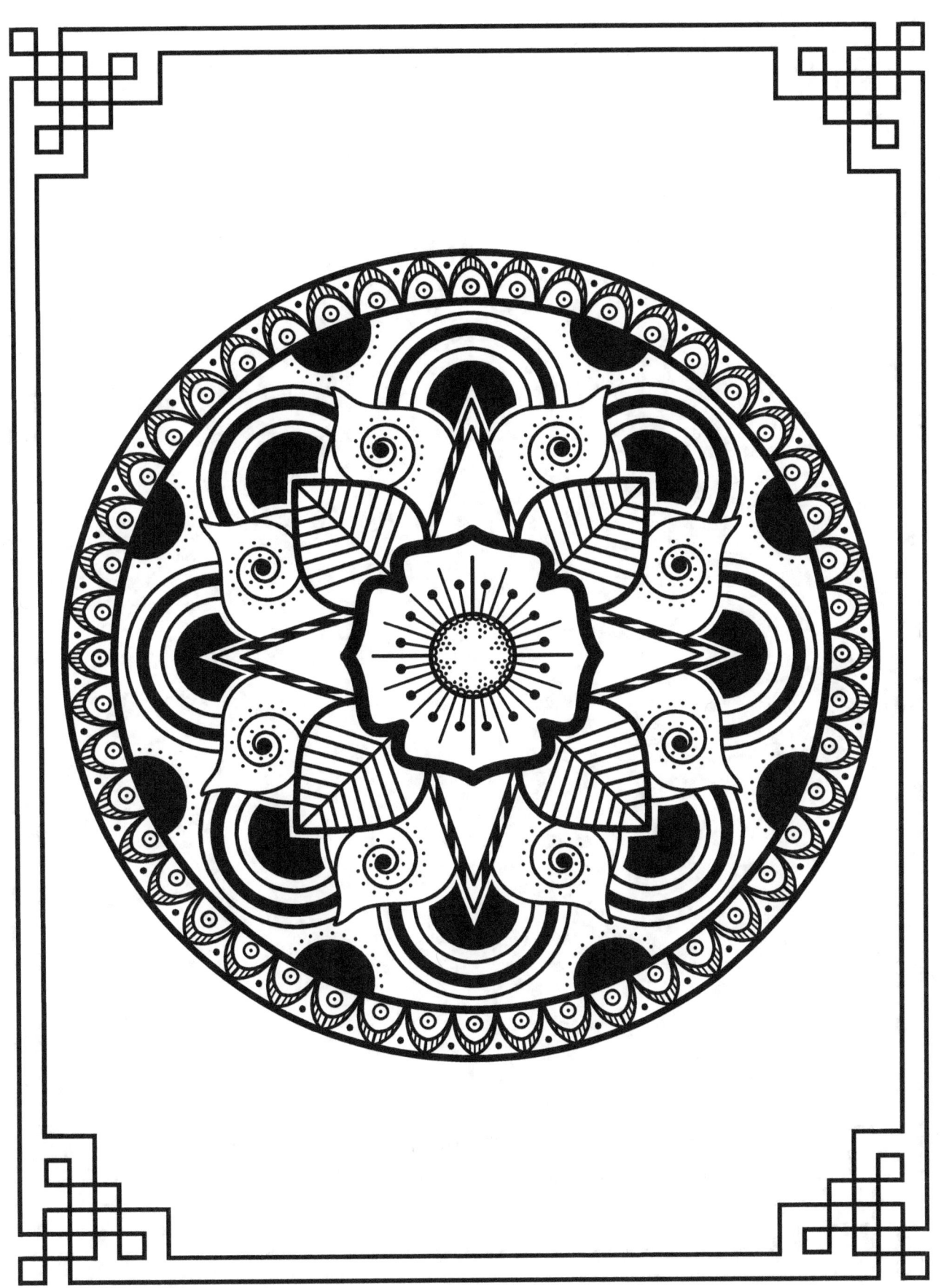

If you have an intention you want to meditate on, you can write it down here.

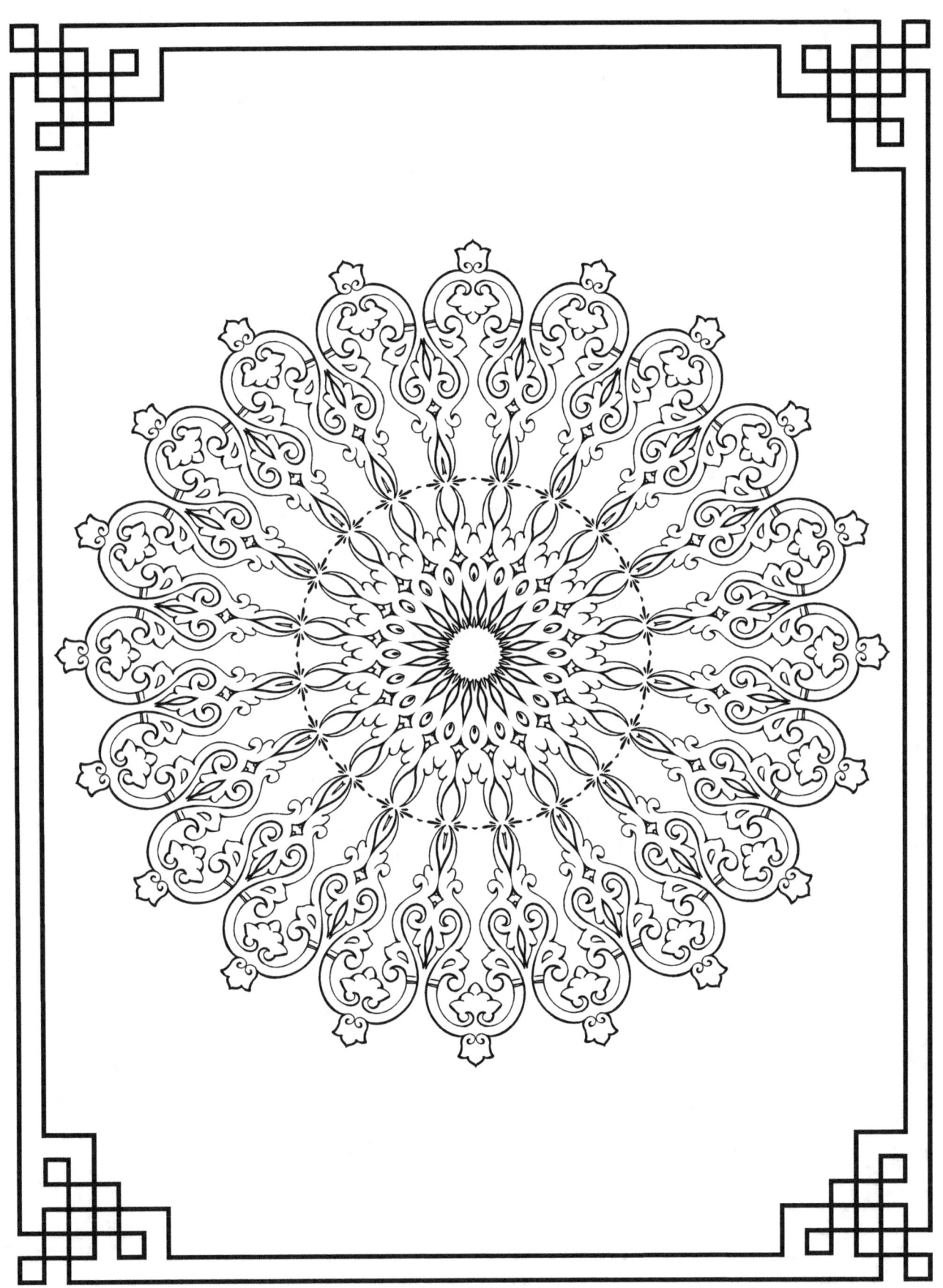

If you have an intention you want to meditate on,
you can write it down here.

If you have an intention you want to meditate on, you can write it down here.

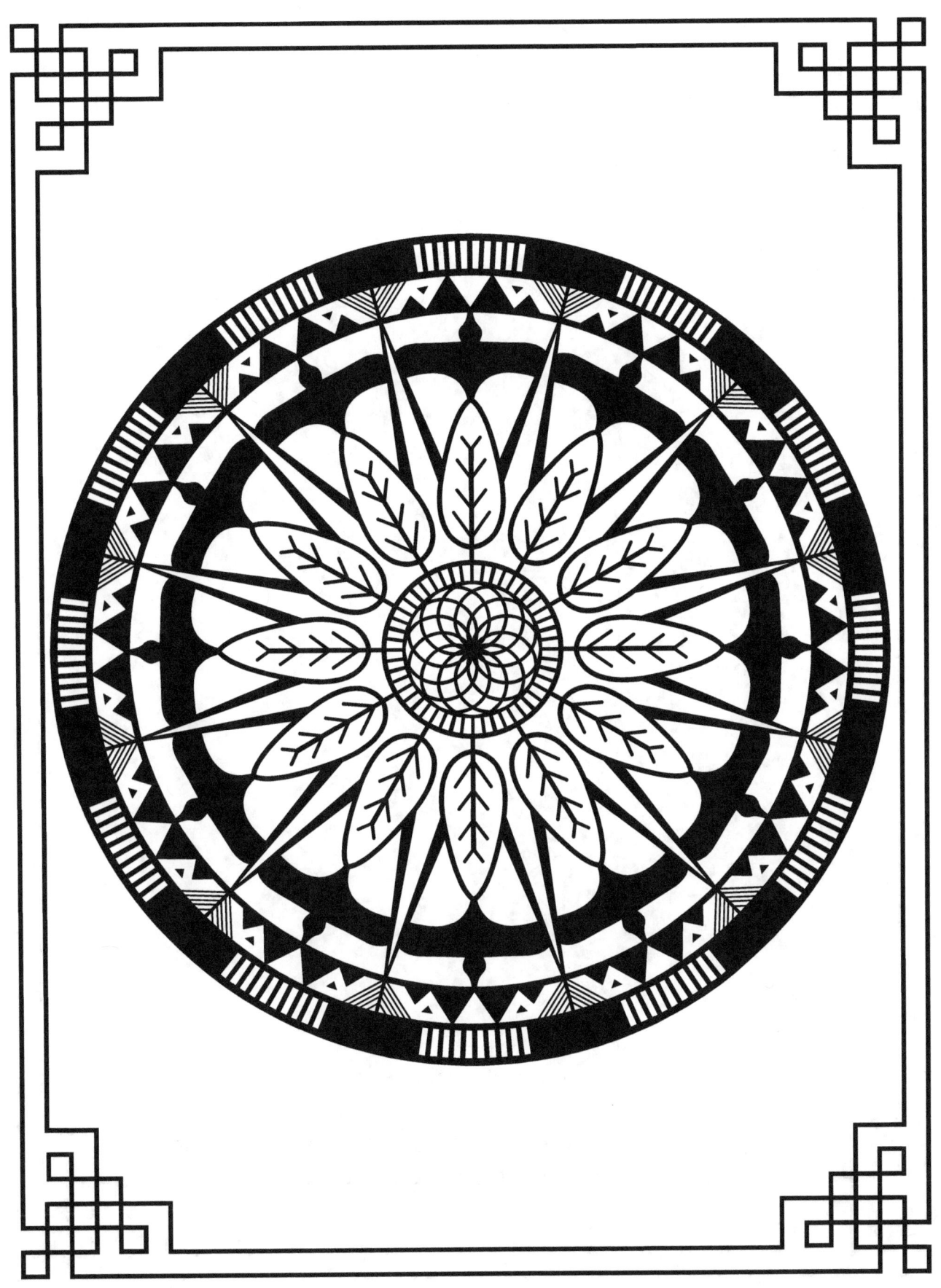

If you have an intention you want to meditate on,
you can write it down here.

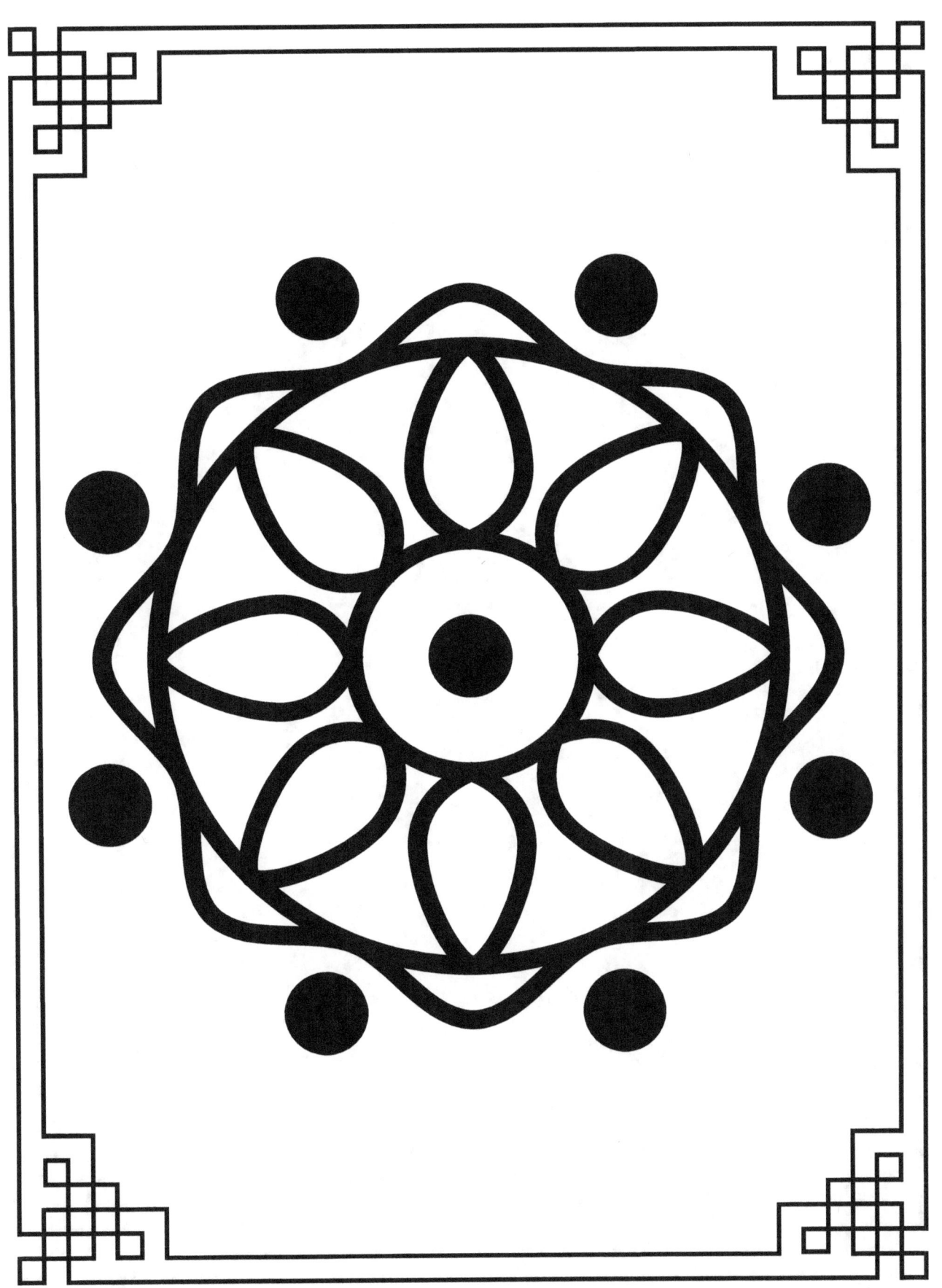

If you have an intention you want to meditate on, you can write it down here.

If you have an intention you want to meditate on,
you can write it down here.

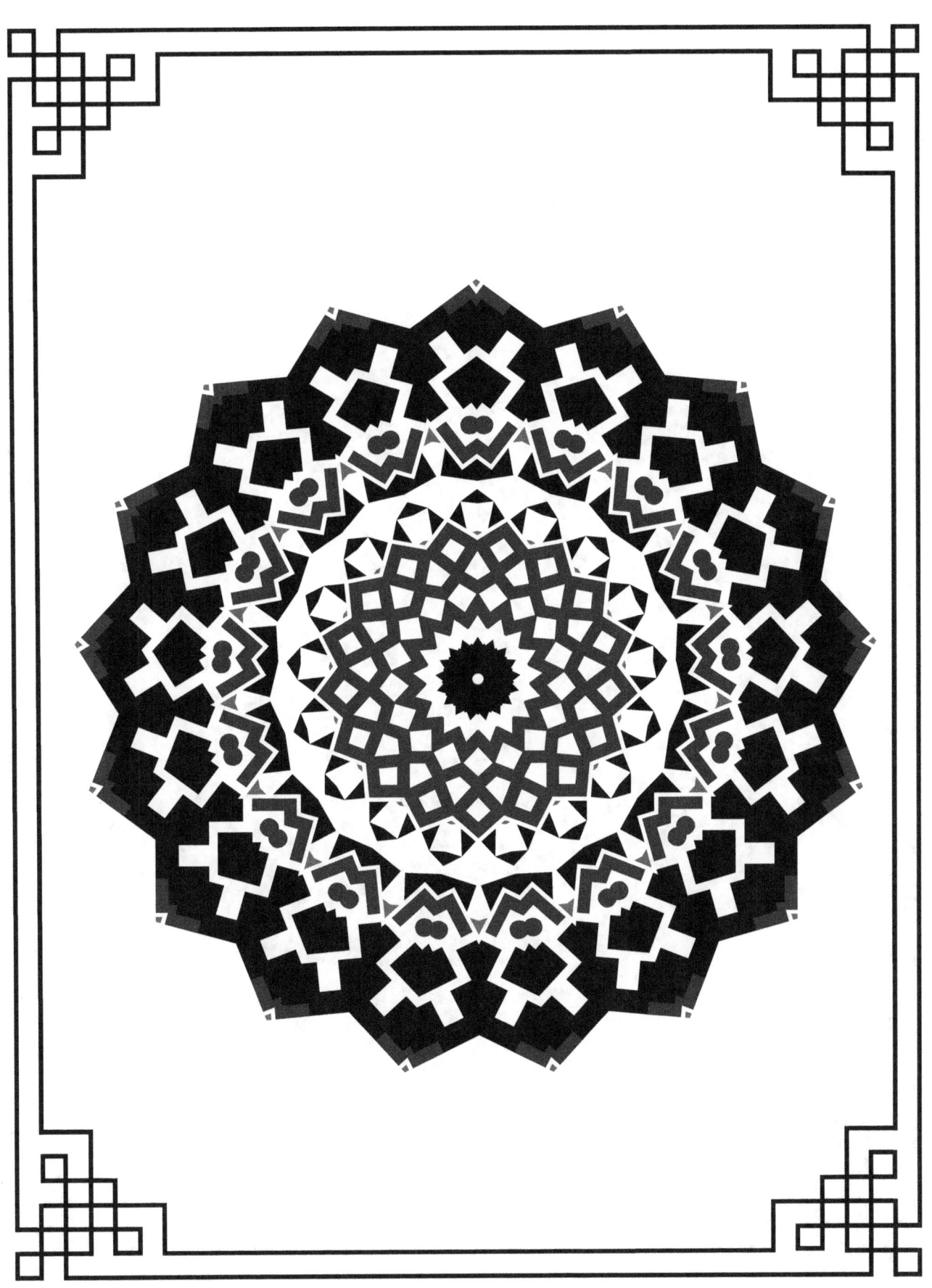

If you have an intention you want to meditate on, you can write it down here.

DRAW YOUR OWN MANDALA HERE.

www.ingramcontent.com/pod-product-compliance
Lightning Source LLC
Chambersburg PA
CBHW081104240526
45465CB00026B/3318